Neovim from Zero to Hero:

Mastering the Ultimate Text Editor

CONTENTS:

- Installing and managing plugins with Packer or Lazy.nvim.
- Exploring themes and color schemes.
- Setting up status lines (e.g., lualine or vim-airline).

Chapter 3: Productivity Features

- Using buffers, tabs, and split windows for multitasking.
- Managing multiple files and projects in Neovim.
- Search and replace with power: grep, fzf, and more.
- Quick navigation with marks, jumps, and folds.
- Working with registers and macros for repetitive tasks.

Chapter 4: Neovim as an IDE

- Understanding Language Server Protocol (LSP) in Neovim.
- Setting up LSP for popular programming languages.
- Installing and configuring autocompletion with nvim-cmp.
- Adding linting and formatting tools (null-ls, Prettier, etc.).
- Debugging with nvim-dap.

Chapter 5: Advanced Plugin Management

- Exploring essential plugins for productivity (e.g., telescope.nvim, treesitter).
- Managing plugin dependencies and ensuring compatibility.
- Optimizing Neovim performance with lazy loading.
- Troubleshooting and resolving plugin conflicts.

Chapter 6: Working with Git in Neovim

- Setting up Git in Neovim.
- Using fugitive.vim and gitsigns.nvim for Git workflows.

- Viewing diffs, staging changes, and committing directly from Neovim.
- Navigating Git blame and logs.

Chapter 7: Writing and Markdown in Neovim

- Setting up Neovim as a writing tool.
- Plugins for writing Markdown (markdown-preview.nvim, vim-pandoc).
- Adding spell check and grammar tools.
- Exporting and previewing Markdown files.

Chapter 8: Exploring Neovim for Templating and Scripting

- Automating workflows with custom commands.
- Setting up snippets for faster coding (e.g., luasnip, ultisnips).
- Writing and running scripts directly in Neovim.

Chapter 9: Neovim for Remote Development

- Accessing remote servers with Neovim (ssh, mosh).
- Using Neovim with Tmux for seamless multitasking.
- Remote file editing with plugins like vim-ftp and rclone.
- Integrating with cloud IDEs and containerized environments.

Chapter 10: Troubleshooting and Debugging Neovim

- Debugging configuration errors in Neovim.
- Using :messages, :checkhealth, and log files for troubleshooting.
- Resolving conflicts between plugins and settings.
- Tips for staying updated with the latest Neovim changes.

Chapter 11: Taking Neovim to the Next Level

- Writing your own plugins in Lua or Vimscript.

- Integrating Neovim with external tools (e.g., fzf, ripgrep).
- Advanced search and replace with Neovim commands.
- Sharing your Neovim configuration on GitHub.

Conclusion:

- Reflecting on your journey from zero to hero.
- The importance of continuous learning with Neovim.
- Resources for staying updated (e.g., communities, forums, GitHub).

Appendices:

- Neovim Cheat Sheet for Quick Reference.
- Recommended Plugins and Configurations.
- FAQs for Beginners and Common Errors.

Neovim from Zero to Hero

Mastering the Ultimate Text Editor

Introduction

A Brief History of Neovim

Neovim emerged as a modern reimagining of the classic Vim editor, a tool cherished by developers for decades due to its speed, versatility, and keyboard-centric workflow. Vim itself is an improved version of Vi, which first appeared in 1976 as part of the Unix operating system. Over time, Vim became a powerful yet complex editor. In 2014, Neovim was introduced as a fork of Vim, with a focus on modernizing its architecture, making it more extensible, and addressing long-standing issues like plugin integration and user interface limitations.

By combining the efficiency of Vim with modern programming paradigms, Neovim has evolved into a robust and flexible tool for coding, writing, and enhancing productivity. Its thriving community and active development ensure that it continues to meet the needs of developers in the fast-paced tech world.

What Makes Neovim Unique?

Neovim stands out due to its core principles of **simplicity**, **extensibility**, and **usability**. Some of the key features that make Neovim so popular among developers include:

- **Asynchronous architecture** for faster and more responsive editing.
- **Lua-based configuration**, offering unparalleled flexibility and ease of scripting.
- A **thriving plugin ecosystem**, allowing users to tailor the editor to their specific needs.
- **Cross-platform support**, making it accessible on various operating systems.
- **Improved UX/UI**, including features like floating windows and better terminal integration.

Neovim is more than just a text editor; it's a powerful platform that can be customized to fit workflows across multiple disciplines.

Why Master Neovim?

Mastering Neovim can transform the way you approach coding, writing, and everyday tasks. Some key benefits include:

- **Efficiency:** Neovim's keyboard-driven navigation eliminates the need for constant mouse usage, saving valuable time.
- **Customizability:** Build your ideal development environment by configuring Neovim to suit your exact preferences.
- **Productivity Boost:** With powerful tools like macros, plugins, and integrated terminals, Neovim enhances your ability to work seamlessly.
- **Portability:** A portable configuration means you can replicate your setup across multiple systems.

- **Community Support:** Join a vibrant community of developers who constantly push the boundaries of what Neovim can achieve.

Who Is This Book For?

This book is designed to cater to users at every skill level:

- **Beginners:** If you're new to Neovim, this book will guide you through the basics, helping you set up and understand the editor's fundamentals.
- **Intermediate Users:** Learn how to optimize your workflow with advanced configurations, plugins, and scripting.
- **Advanced Users:** Dive into the intricacies of Neovim's architecture, develop custom plugins, and fine-tune your setup for ultimate performance.

Overview of This Book

This book is structured to provide a comprehensive learning experience:

- ✓ **Getting Started:** Setting up Neovim and understanding its core concepts.
- ✓ **Essential Commands and Navigation:** Mastering the basics for efficient text editing.
- ✓ **Customization and Configuration:** Tailoring Neovim to suit your workflow with Lua.
- ✓ **Plugins and Extensions:** Exploring must-have plugins and building your own extensions.
- ✓ **Advanced Techniques:** Delving into advanced features like LSP (Language Server Protocol) integration and debugging.
- ✓ **Practical Use Cases:** Applying Neovim to real-world coding, writing, and productivity tasks.

✓ **Tips, Tricks, and Resources:** Hidden features, community resources, and ongoing learning opportunities.

Chapter 1: Getting Started with Neovim

What is Neovim, and Why Should You Use It?

Neovim is a modernized fork of Vim, one of the most powerful and enduring text editors in the programming world. While Vim is renowned for its efficiency and minimalism, Neovim builds on this foundation by introducing modern features such as asynchronous operations, enhanced plugin support, and Lua-based scripting.

Neovim empowers developers, writers, and tech enthusiasts to work faster, more efficiently, and with greater customization. If you're tired of bulky IDEs or simply looking for a text editor that can adapt to your workflow, Neovim offers a compelling alternative.

Installing Neovim on Different Platforms

The first step to mastering Neovim is installing it on your system. Neovim is cross-platform and can be set up on Windows, macOS, and Linux.

Windows

1. **Download Neovim:** Visit the official Neovim releases page and download the latest `.zip` file for Windows.

2. **Extract the Archive:** Extract the contents to a folder of your choice (e.g., `C:\Neovim`).
3. **Add to Path:**
   - Open "Environment Variables" on your system.
   - Add the path to Neovim's `bin` folder (e.g., `C:\Neovim\bin`) to the `Path` variable.
4. **Verify Installation:** Open Command Prompt or PowerShell and type `nvim`. If Neovim launches, you're good to go.

macOS

1. **Using Homebrew:**

```bash
CopierModifier
brew install neovim
```

2. **Verify Installation:** Run `nvim` in the terminal to ensure Neovim is installed.

Linux

1. **Using Package Managers:**
   - **Debian/Ubuntu:**

```bash
CopierModifier
sudo apt update
sudo apt install neovim
```

   - **Fedora:**

```bash
CopierModifier
sudo dnf install neovim
```

o **Arch Linux:**

```bash
CopierModifier
sudo pacman -S neovim
```

2. **Verify Installation:** Run `nvim` in the terminal.

For other installation methods or prebuilt binaries, visit the official documentation.

Setting Up Your First Configuration File

Once Neovim is installed, you'll need to configure it to match your preferences. Neovim reads configuration files from:

- **Linux/macOS:** `~/.config/nvim/init.lua`
- **Windows:** `%LOCALAPPDATA%\nvim\init.lua`

If you're familiar with Vim, you can use a `.vimrc` file instead. However, Neovim's preferred configuration language is Lua, as it offers better performance and flexibility.

Creating Your `init.lua`

1. **Create the Configuration File:**

```bash
CopierModifier
mkdir -p ~/.config/nvim
touch ~/.config/nvim/init.lua
```

2. **Add Basic Settings:** Open the file in Neovim and add the following:

```
lua
CopierModifier
-- Enable line numbers
vim.opt.number = true

-- Set relative line numbers
vim.opt.relativenumber = true

-- Enable syntax highlighting
vim.cmd("syntax on")

-- Set tab width
vim.opt.tabstop = 4
vim.opt.shiftwidth = 4
vim.opt.expandtab = true
```

Using a `.vimrc` File (Optional)

If you prefer Vim-style configuration, you can create a `.vimrc` file and use it in Neovim. Simply place the file in your home directory and add your desired settings.

Navigating Neovim: Basic Modes

Neovim, like Vim, operates in different modes. Mastering these is key to efficient editing.

- **Normal Mode:** Default mode for navigation and commands. Press `Esc` to return to normal mode.
- **Insert Mode:** For editing text. Enter insert mode by pressing `i` or `a`. Exit by pressing `Esc`.
- **Visual Mode:** For selecting text. Activate with `v` (character-wise), `V` (line-wise), or `Ctrl+v` (block-wise).
- **Command-Line Mode:** For executing commands. Enter this mode by pressing `:`.

Essential Commands to Start Editing

Here are some fundamental commands to help you get started:

File Operations

- **Open a file:** `:e filename`
- **Save a file:** `:w`
- **Save and quit:** `:wq` or `:x`
- **Quit without saving:** `:q!`

Navigation

- **Move to the beginning of a line:** `0`
- **Move to the end of a line:** `$`
- **Move one word forward:** `w`
- **Move one word backward:** `b`

Editing

- **Delete a character:** `x`
- **Delete a word:** `dw`
- **Undo a change:** `u`
- **Redo a change:** `Ctrl+r`

Searching

- **Search for a word:** `/word`
- **Repeat search forward:** `n`
- **Repeat search backward:** `N`

By mastering these basics, you'll be well on your way to unlocking Neovim's potential. In the next chapter, we'll dive deeper into commands and navigation for a more efficient editing experience.

Chapter 2: Customizing Neovim

Customization is one of Neovim's greatest strengths. With Lua as its preferred configuration language, Neovim provides a modern, efficient, and flexible way to tailor your editor to your needs. This chapter will guide you through customizing key bindings, installing plugins, and enhancing the visual appeal of your setup.

Introduction to Lua-Based Configuration in Neovim

While traditional Vim used the `.vimrc` file for configuration, Neovim supports Lua, enabling more powerful and cleaner configurations. Lua scripts are faster to execute, more readable, and offer advanced features for plugin management and scripting.

Why Lua?

- **Performance:** Lua executes faster than Vimscript.
- **Readability:** Lua syntax is simpler and easier to understand.
- **Extensibility:** Lua allows for deeper integration with plugins and Neovim features.

To start customizing Neovim with Lua, edit the `init.lua` file in your configuration directory:

- **Linux/macOS:** `~/.config/nvim/init.lua`
- **Windows:** `%LOCALAPPDATA%\nvim\init.lua`

Example of a basic Lua configuration:

```lua
CopierModifier
-- General settings
vim.opt.number = true          -- Enable line
numbers
vim.opt.relativenumber = true -- Show relative
line numbers

-- Key mappings
vim.g.mapleader = " "          -- Set space as the
leader key
vim.keymap.set('n', '<leader>w', ':w<CR>') --
Save with <leader>w

-- Enable mouse support
vim.opt.mouse = 'a'
```

Customizing Key Bindings

Key bindings allow you to enhance your workflow by assigning frequently used actions to simple key combinations.

Setting Key Bindings in Lua

You can define key bindings using the `vim.keymap.set` function. The format is:

```lua
CopierModifier
vim.keymap.set(mode, keys, action, options)
```

- **mode**: Specifies the mode (n for normal, i for insert, etc.).
- **keys**: The key combination.
- **action**: The command or function to execute.
- **options**: Optional parameters like silent execution.

Example key bindings:

```lua
CopierModifier
-- Save file with <leader>s
vim.keymap.set('n', '<leader>s', ':w<CR>')

-- Quit Neovim with <leader>q
vim.keymap.set('n', '<leader>q', ':q<CR>')

-- Quickly open the init.lua file
vim.keymap.set('n', '<leader>e', ':e
~/.config/nvim/init.lua<CR>')
```

These customizations make everyday actions faster and more intuitive.

Installing and Managing Plugins

Plugins are a core part of Neovim's customization. With modern plugin managers like **Packer** or **Lazy.nvim**, you can install, update, and remove plugins effortlessly.

Installing Packer

1. **Install Packer:**

   ```bash
   CopierModifier
   ```

```
git clone --depth 1
https://github.com/wbthomason/packer.nvim
\
~/.local/share/nvim/site/pack/packer/start
/packer.nvim
```

2. **Basic Packer Configuration:** Add the following to your `init.lua`:

```lua
CopierModifier
-- Load Packer
vim.cmd([[packadd packer.nvim]])

-- Plugins
require('packer').startup(function(use)
    use 'wbthomason/packer.nvim' -- Packer
manages itself
end)
```

3. **Adding Plugins:** List plugins in the `startup` function. For example:

```lua
CopierModifier
require('packer').startup(function(use)
    use 'nvim-treesitter/nvim-treesitter'
-- Syntax highlighting
    use 'nvim-lua/plenary.nvim'
-- Utility library
    use 'tpope/vim-fugitive'            -
- Git integration
end)
```

4. **Install Plugins:** Open Neovim and run `:PackerSync`.

Lazy.nvim (Alternative Plugin Manager)

Lazy.nvim is another excellent plugin manager, focusing on lazy loading for performance. Visit the Lazy.nvim GitHub page for installation instructions.

Exploring Themes and Color Schemes

Neovim supports various themes and color schemes to enhance readability and aesthetics.

Installing a Theme

Add a theme plugin to your plugin manager. For example:

```lua
CopierModifier
use 'gruvbox-community/gruvbox' -- Gruvbox theme
```

Setting a Theme

After installing a theme, activate it in your configuration:

```lua
CopierModifier
vim.cmd([[colorscheme gruvbox]])
```

Popular themes include:

- **Gruvbox**: A retro-inspired color scheme.
- **Dracula**: A dark theme with vibrant colors.
- **Nord**: A theme inspired by the Arctic.

Setting Up Status Lines

A custom status line can display useful information like file name, position, and mode. Popular plugins for this are **lualine** and **vim-airline**.

Lualine

1. **Install Lualine:**

   ```lua
   CopierModifier
   use 'nvim-lualine/lualine.nvim'
   use 'nvim-tree/nvim-web-devicons' -- Optional, for icons
   ```

2. **Configure Lualine:**

   ```lua
   CopierModifier
   require('lualine').setup {
       options = {
           theme = 'gruvbox', -- Match your chosen theme
           section_separators = '',
           component_separators = ''
       }
   }
   ```

Vim-Airline

For users preferring Vimscript-based configuration, vim-airline is an excellent alternative.

By the end of this chapter, you should have a fully customized Neovim setup that enhances your productivity and fits your style. In the next chapter, we'll explore advanced navigation and editing techniques to take your Neovim skills to the next level.

Chapter 3: Productivity Features

Neovim is designed to enhance your productivity, offering tools and workflows for efficient multitasking, navigation, and file management. This chapter will explore its powerful productivity features, helping you make the most of your time while coding or writing.

Using Buffers, Tabs, and Split Windows for Multitasking

Buffers: The Core of Multitasking

Buffers are open files or scratch areas in Neovim. Unlike traditional tabs in other editors, buffers are not tied to a specific visual tab. You can think of buffers as the foundation for managing multiple files.

- **List Buffers:** `:ls` or `:buffers`
- **Switch Buffers:**
    - `:b<number>` (e.g., `:b2` to switch to buffer 2)
    - `:bnext` or `:bn` to go to the next buffer.

- o : `:bprevious` or `:bp` to go to the previous buffer.
- **Delete a Buffer:** `:bd` (buffer delete)

Example key bindings for buffer navigation:

```lua
CopierModifier
vim.keymap.set('n', '<leader>bn', ':bnext<CR>')
vim.keymap.set('n', '<leader>bp',
':bprevious<CR>')
vim.keymap.set('n', '<leader>bd', ':bd<CR>')
```

Tabs: Grouping Buffers

Tabs in Neovim are more like "workspaces" that can contain multiple windows.

- **New Tab:** `:tabnew` or `:tabnew <filename>`
- **Switch Tabs:**
  - o : `:tabnext` or `gt` to go to the next tab.
  - o : `:tabprevious` or `gT` to go to the previous tab.
- **Close Tab:** `:tabclose`

Split Windows: A Flexible Layout

Splits allow you to view multiple files or sections of a file simultaneously.

- **Horizontal Split:** `:split` or `:sp <filename>`
- **Vertical Split:** `:vsplit` or `:vs <filename>`
- **Switch Between Splits:**
  - o `<Ctrl-w><h/j/k/l>` to move left, down, up, or right.
- **Resize Splits:**

o   `:resize +N` or `:resize -N` to increase/decrease height.

o   `:vertical resize +N` or `:vertical resize -N` to adjust width.

Example key bindings for splits:

```lua
CopierModifier
vim.keymap.set('n', '<leader>sh', ':split<CR>')
vim.keymap.set('n', '<leader>sv', ':vsplit<CR>')
vim.keymap.set('n', '<leader>sc', '<C-w>c') --
Close split
vim.keymap.set('n', '<leader>se', '<C-w>=') --
Equalize split sizes
```

Managing Multiple Files and Projects

File Explorer Plugins

Install a file explorer like **nvim-tree** for a visual directory structure.

1. **Install Plugin:**

   ```lua
   CopierModifier
   use 'nvim-tree/nvim-tree.lua'
   ```

2. **Setup:**

   ```lua
   CopierModifier
   require('nvim-tree').setup()
   vim.keymap.set('n', '<leader>e',
   ':NvimTreeToggle<CR>') -- Toggle file tree
   ```

Project Management with Telescope

Telescope is a highly extensible fuzzy finder for managing files, buffers, and more.

1. **Install Telescope:**

```lua
lua
CopierModifier
use {
    'nvim-telescope/telescope.nvim',
    requires = { 'nvim-lua/plenary.nvim' }
}
```

2. **Key Bindings:**

```lua
lua
CopierModifier
vim.keymap.set('n', '<leader>ff',
':Telescope find_files<CR>')
vim.keymap.set('n', '<leader>fg',
':Telescope live_grep<CR>')
vim.keymap.set('n', '<leader>fb',
':Telescope buffers<CR>')
vim.keymap.set('n', '<leader>fh',
':Telescope help_tags<CR>')
```

Search and Replace with Power: Grep, FZF, and More

Built-in Search and Replace

- **Search:** /pattern (forward) or ?pattern (backward)
- **Replace:**

```vim
vim
CopierModifier
:%s/old/new/g     " Replace all occurrences
in the file
```

```
:%s/old/new/gc    " Replace with
confirmation
```

External Tools: Grep and Ripgrep

You can integrate external tools for advanced searches.

- **Search Files with Grep:**

```vim
CopierModifier
:grep "pattern" .
:copen            " Open the quickfix list
```

Fuzzy Search with FZF

Install **fzf.vim** for lightning-fast file searches.

```lua
CopierModifier
use { 'junegunn/fzf.vim', run = ':fzf#install()'
}
vim.keymap.set('n', '<leader>p', ':Files<CR>')
```

Quick Navigation with Marks, Jumps, and Folds

Marks

Marks allow you to save positions in files.

- **Set a Mark:** m<letter> (e.g., ma sets mark a)
- **Jump to a Mark:** 'a

Jumps

Navigate through your editing history using jumps.

- **Go Back:** `<C-o>`
- **Go Forward:** `<C-i>`

Folds

Folds let you collapse and expand sections of a file.

- **Create Fold:** `zf` followed by a motion (e.g., `zf%` for a block).
- **Toggle Fold:** `za`

Working with Registers and Macros

Registers

Registers store text for copy-paste operations.

- **Yank to a Register:** `"ay` (yanks to register `a`)
- **Paste from a Register:** `"ap`

Macros

Macros automate repetitive tasks by recording and replaying commands.

- **Start Recording:** `q<letter>` (e.g., `qa` starts recording in register `a`)
- **Stop Recording:** `q`
- **Replay Macro:** `@<letter>`

Example: Recording a macro to append `;` to the end of each line:

1. `qa` (start recording in register `a`).

2. `A;` (append `;` at the end of the line).
3. `j` (move to the next line).
4. `q` (stop recording).
5. `@a` (replay the macro).

Chapter 4: Neovim as an IDE

Neovim has evolved far beyond a text editor, offering features and tools that rival modern Integrated Development Environments (IDEs). With support for the Language Server Protocol (LSP), autocompletion, linting, and debugging, Neovim can be transformed into a fully functional IDE tailored to your workflow.

Understanding Language Server Protocol (LSP) in Neovim

The Language Server Protocol (LSP) is a standardized way to enable features like autocompletion, go-to-definition, hover documentation, and more. Neovim provides built-in LSP support via the `nvim-lspconfig` plugin.

How LSP Works:

1. **Language Servers**: Provide programming language-specific features.
2. **Neovim LSP Client**: Communicates with the server to deliver functionality to the user.

Setting Up LSP for Popular Programming Languages

Install the `nvim-lspconfig` plugin for managing LSP servers:

```lua
lua
CopierModifier
use 'neovim/nvim-lspconfig'
```

Example: Setting Up LSP for Python

1. **Install Python LSP Server:**

   ```bash
   bash
   CopierModifier
   pip install python-lsp-server
   ```

2. **Configure Neovim:**

   ```lua
   lua
   CopierModifier
   require('lspconfig').pylsp.setup {}
   ```

Example: Setting Up LSP for JavaScript/TypeScript

1. **Install TypeScript LSP Server:**

   ```bash
   bash
   CopierModifier
   npm install -g typescript-language-server typescript
   ```

2. **Configure Neovim:**

   ```lua
   lua
   ```

```
CopierModifier
require('lspconfig').tsserver.setup {}
```

Key Bindings for LSP Features

Add key bindings for common LSP actions:

```lua
CopierModifier
vim.keymap.set('n', 'gd',
vim.lsp.buf.definition, { desc = 'Go to
Definition' })
vim.keymap.set('n', 'K', vim.lsp.buf.hover, {
desc = 'Hover Documentation' })
vim.keymap.set('n', '<leader>rn',
vim.lsp.buf.rename, { desc = 'Rename Symbol' })
```

Installing and Configuring Autocompletion with nvim-cmp

Autocompletion is essential for productivity. Use the nvim-cmp plugin for a seamless autocompletion experience.

Install the Plugin:

```lua
CopierModifier
use {
    'hrsh7th/nvim-cmp',
    requires = {
        'hrsh7th/cmp-nvim-lsp',
        'hrsh7th/cmp-buffer',
        'hrsh7th/cmp-path',
        'hrsh7th/cmp-cmdline',
        'L3MON4D3/LuaSnip'
    }
}
```

Configure nvim-cmp:

```lua
CopierModifier
local cmp = require('cmp')
cmp.setup {
    snippet = {
        expand = function(args)

require('luasnip').lsp_expand(args.body)
        end,
    },
    mapping = {
        ['<Tab>'] =
cmp.mapping.select_next_item(),
        ['<S-Tab>'] =
cmp.mapping.select_prev_item(),
        ['<CR>'] = cmp.mapping.confirm { select
= true },
    },
    sources = cmp.config.sources {
        { name = 'nvim_lsp' },
        { name = 'buffer' },
        { name = 'path' },
    },
}
```

Adding Linting and Formatting Tools

Linting and formatting improve code quality and
readability. Tools like `null-ls` integrate seamlessly with
Neovim.

Install `null-ls`:

```lua
CopierModifier
use {
    'jose-elias-alvarez/null-ls.nvim',
    requires = { 'nvim-lua/plenary.nvim' }
}
```

Configure `null-ls` for Formatting and Linting:

```lua
CopierModifier
local null_ls = require('null-ls')
null_ls.setup {
    sources = {
        null_ls.builtins.formatting.prettier,
        null_ls.builtins.diagnostics.eslint,
    },
}
```

Example: Key Binding for Formatting

```lua
CopierModifier
vim.keymap.set('n', '<leader>f',
vim.lsp.buf.format, { desc = 'Format Code' })
```

Debugging with `nvim-dap`

Debugging is crucial for any developer. Neovim supports debugging via the `nvim-dap` plugin.

Install the Plugin:

```lua
CopierModifier
use {
    'mfussenegger/nvim-dap',
    requires = { 'rcarriga/nvim-dap-ui' }
}
```

Configure `nvim-dap`:

1. **Set Up Adapters:**

   ```lua
   CopierModifier
   ```

```lua
local dap = require('dap')
dap.adapters.python = {
    type = 'executable',
    command = 'python',
    args = { '-m', 'debugpy.adapter' },
}
dap.configurations.python = {
    {
        type = 'python',
        request = 'launch',
        program = '${file}',
        pythonPath = function()
            return '/usr/bin/python'
        end,
    },
}
```

2. **Enable Debugger UI:**

```lua
CopierModifier
require('dapui').setup()
```

Key Bindings for Debugging:

```lua
CopierModifier
vim.keymap.set('n', '<F5>', dap.continue, { desc
= 'Start/Continue Debugging' })
vim.keymap.set('n', '<F10>', dap.step_over, {
desc = 'Step Over' })
vim.keymap.set('n', '<F11>', dap.step_into, {
desc = 'Step Into' })
vim.keymap.set('n', '<F12>', dap.step_out, {
desc = 'Step Out' })
```

By the end of this chapter, you'll have transformed Neovim into a powerful IDE, equipped with tools for LSP, autocompletion, linting, formatting, and debugging. In the next chapter, we'll explore advanced text editing techniques to further enhance your Neovim expertise.

Chapter 5: Advanced Plugin Management

Neovim's plugin ecosystem is vast and powerful, allowing you to tailor your editor for ultimate productivity. This chapter dives into essential plugins, techniques for managing dependencies, optimizing performance, and troubleshooting common issues.

Exploring Essential Plugins for Productivity

The right plugins can elevate your Neovim experience, enabling faster workflows and enhanced functionality. Below are some must-have plugins:

1. Telescope.nvim (Fuzzy Finder)

Telescope is a powerful fuzzy finder that makes navigating files, searching content, and running commands effortless.

```
lua
CopierModifier
use {
    'nvim-telescope/telescope.nvim',
    requires = { 'nvim-lua/plenary.nvim' }
}
```

- **Key Features**: File searching, live grep, and workspace navigation.
- **Example Key Binding**:

```lua
CopierModifier
vim.keymap.set('n', '<leader>ff',
'<cmd>Telescope find_files<CR>', { desc =
'Find Files' })
vim.keymap.set('n', '<leader>fg',
'<cmd>Telescope live_grep<CR>', { desc =
'Live Grep' })
```

2. nvim-treesitter (Code Parsing and Highlighting)

Treesitter provides better syntax highlighting, code navigation, and text objects by parsing code in a more accurate manner.

```lua
CopierModifier
use {
    'nvim-treesitter/nvim-treesitter',
    run = ':TSUpdate'
}
```

- **Key Features**: Enhanced syntax highlighting, folding, and code-aware selections.
- **Setup Example**:

```lua
CopierModifier
require('nvim-treesitter.configs').setup {
    ensure_installed = 'all',
    highlight = { enable = true },
    incremental_selection = { enable =
true },
}
```

3. Comment.nvim (Efficient Commenting)

A plugin to quickly toggle comments for code.

```lua
CopierModifier
use 'numToStr/Comment.nvim'
```

- **Key Binding Example**:

  ```lua
  CopierModifier
  require('Comment').setup()
  vim.keymap.set('n', '<leader>/', '<cmd>lua
  require("Comment.api").toggle.linewise.cur
  rent()<CR>', { desc = 'Toggle Comment' })
  ```

Managing Plugin Dependencies and Ensuring Compatibility

1. Using Dependency Managers

Plugins often depend on libraries or other plugins. Dependency management is automatic with tools like `packer.nvim`.

- Example with Dependencies:

  ```lua
  CopierModifier
  use {
      'nvim-telescope/telescope-fzf-
  native.nvim',
      run = 'make',
      requires = { 'nvim-
  telescope/telescope.nvim' }
  }
  ```

2. Pinning Plugin Versions

To avoid breaking changes, pin plugins to a specific version:

```lua
CopierModifier
use { 'nvim-lualine/lualine.nvim', commit =
'a1b2c3d' }
```

3. Checking Compatibility

- **Neovim Version Requirements**: Review plugin documentation to ensure compatibility with your Neovim version.
- **GitHub Issues**: Check for open issues to identify known bugs or conflicts.

Optimizing Neovim Performance with Lazy Loading

Lazy loading plugins can significantly reduce startup time by only loading plugins when needed.

Lazy Loading Examples

1. **Load on Specific File Types**:

   ```lua
   CopierModifier
   use {
       'lukas-reineke/indent-blankline.nvim',
       ft = { 'python', 'javascript' }
   }
   ```

2. **Load on Specific Commands**:

```lua
CopierModifier
use {
    'kyazdani42/nvim-tree.lua',
    cmd = 'NvimTreeToggle'
}
```

3. **Load on Specific Events**:

```lua
CopierModifier
use {
    'lewis6991/gitsigns.nvim',
    event = 'BufRead'
}
```

Monitor Startup Performance

Use the `startup.nvim` plugin to analyze and optimize Neovim's startup time.

```lua
CopierModifier
use 'dstein64/vim-startuptime'
```

Run the command:

```vim
CopierModifier
:StartupTime
```

Troubleshooting and Resolving Plugin Conflicts

1. Identify Conflicting Plugins

- **Common Symptoms**: Errors on startup, broken key mappings, or unexpected behavior.
- **Debugging Steps**:

o Disable plugins one by one to identify the culprit.
o Use `:checkhealth` to detect issues with popular plugins like LSP and Treesitter.

2. Check Plugin Logs

Many plugins provide verbose logging options for debugging. For example, `nvim-lspconfig` logs errors with:

```lua
CopierModifier
vim.lsp.set_log_level('debug')
```

3. Fallback to Minimal Config

Run Neovim with minimal configuration to isolate problems:

```bash
CopierModifier
nvim -u NONE
```

4. Updating Plugins

Ensure plugins are up-to-date:

```lua
CopierModifier
:PackerUpdate
```

By mastering advanced plugin management, you can unlock the full potential of Neovim while ensuring a smooth, optimized experience. The next chapter will dive deeper into collaborative and remote workflows using Neovim, focusing on tools for pair programming and version control integration.

Chapter 6: Working with Git in Neovim

Neovim's flexibility allows developers to integrate powerful Git workflows directly into their editor, streamlining version control and boosting productivity. This chapter covers how to set up Git in Neovim, use essential plugins, and perform common Git tasks without leaving your workspace.

Setting Up Git in Neovim

Before diving into plugins, ensure Git is installed on your system:

- **Check Installation**:

  ```bash
  CopierModifier
  git --version
  ```

- **Configure Git**:

  ```bash
  CopierModifier
  git config --global user.name "Your Name"
  git config --global user.email
  "your.email@example.com"
  ```

While Neovim doesn't have built-in Git functionality, plugins like `fugitive.vim` and `gitsigns.nvim` seamlessly integrate Git into your workflow.

Using Fugitive.vim for Git Workflows

Fugitive.vim is a powerful plugin that transforms Neovim into a Git client. It provides commands for staging, committing, and viewing repository information.

Installation

Using `packer.nvim`:

```lua
CopierModifier
use 'tpope/vim-fugitive'
```

Key Fugitive Commands

1. **Open the Git Status Window**:

   ```vim
   CopierModifier
   :Git
   ```

   View staged, unstaged, and untracked files.

2. **Stage a File**:

   ```vim
   CopierModifier
   :Git add %
   ```

   Stages the current file.

3. **Commit Changes**:

```
vim
CopierModifier
:Git commit
```

Opens a commit message buffer.

4. **Push Changes**:

```
vim
CopierModifier
:Git push
```

5. **View a File's Git History**:

```
vim
CopierModifier
:Git log
```

Viewing Diffs with Fugitive

To see changes between the working directory and the index:

```
vim
CopierModifier
:Git diff
```

Using Gitsigns.nvim for Enhanced Git Integration

Gitsigns.nvim provides real-time Git diff indicators in the sign column and offers utilities like inline blame and hunk management.

Installation

Using `packer.nvim`:

```lua
CopierModifier
use {
    'lewis6991/gitsigns.nvim',
    requires = { 'nvim-lua/plenary.nvim' }
}
```

Configuration

```lua
CopierModifier
require('gitsigns').setup {
    signs = {
        add          = { text = '+' },
        change       = { text = '~' },
        delete       = { text = '_' },
        topdelete    = { text = '‾' },
        changedelete = { text = '~' },
    },
    current_line_blame = true, -- Enable inline blame
    on_attach = function(bufnr)
        local gs = package.loaded.gitsigns
        local map = vim.api.nvim_buf_set_keymap
        local opts = { noremap = true, silent = true }
        map(bufnr, 'n', '<leader>hs', '<cmd>lua gs.stage_hunk()<CR>', opts)
        map(bufnr, 'n', '<leader>hu', '<cmd>lua gs.undo_stage_hunk()<CR>', opts)
        map(bufnr, 'n', '<leader>hr', '<cmd>lua gs.reset_hunk()<CR>', opts)
        map(bufnr, 'n', '<leader>hb', '<cmd>lua gs.blame_line()<CR>', opts)
    end
}
```

Key Features of Gitsigns.nvim

1. **Inline Git Signs**: Shows where lines were added, changed, or removed.
2. **Stage or Reset Hunks**:
    o Stage the current hunk:

    ```vim
    CopierModifier
    :Gitsigns stage_hunk
    ```

    o Reset the current hunk:

    ```vim
    CopierModifier
    :Gitsigns reset_hunk
    ```

3. **Blame Lines**:
    o Show inline blame for the current line:

    ```vim
    CopierModifier
    :Gitsigns blame_line
    ```

Viewing Diffs, Staging Changes, and Committing

Viewing Diffs

- **With Fugitive**:

```vim
CopierModifier
:Git diff
```

- **With Gitsigns**:
  Navigate through changes using:

```vim
CopierModifier
]c  -- Next change
```

```
[c  -- Previous change
```

Staging Changes

- **With Fugitive**:

```
vim
CopierModifier
:Git add %
```

- **With Gitsigns**:

```
vim
CopierModifier
:Gitsigns stage_hunk
```

Committing Changes

- Open a commit message buffer:

```
vim
CopierModifier
:Git commit
```

Navigating Git Blame and Logs

Git Blame

- **Inline Blame with Gitsigns**:
  Inline blame shows commit details for the current line.

```
lua
CopierModifier
require('gitsigns').setup {
current_line_blame = true }
```

- **Fugitive Blame Window**:

```vim
CopierModifier
:Git blame
```

Opens a split showing blame details for each line.

Viewing Git Logs

- **With Fugitive**:

```vim
CopierModifier
:Git log
```

- **Jump to Specific Commits**:

```vim
CopierModifier
:Git checkout <commit-hash>
```

With tools like Fugitive and Gitsigns, Neovim becomes a powerful Git client, allowing you to manage version control efficiently without leaving the editor. In the next chapter, we'll explore collaborative tools and techniques for working with remote teams using Neovim.

Chapter 7: Writing and Markdown in Neovim

Neovim isn't just for coding—it's also a versatile tool for writers, bloggers, and anyone working with Markdown files. By configuring Neovim for writing and Markdown editing, you can enjoy a distraction-free workspace, rich with helpful features like spell check, live previews, and export tools.

Setting Up Neovim as a Writing Tool

A clean and distraction-free interface is crucial for writing. Here are some tips for configuring Neovim for writing:

1. **Use a Minimal Theme**:
   Install a theme like `gruvbox` or `catppuccin` for a pleasant writing experience.

   ```lua
   CopierModifier
   use 'ellisonleao/gruvbox.nvim'
   ```

2. **Enable Line Wrapping**:
   For writing prose, enable soft line wrapping:

```
vim
CopierModifier
set wrap
```

3. **Increase Line Spacing**:
   Add some spacing between lines:

```
vim
CopierModifier
set linespace=2
```

4. **Disable Line Numbers and Cursorline**:
   Writing often benefits from a clutter-free screen:

```
vim
CopierModifier
set nonumber norelativenumber nocursorline
```

Plugins for Writing Markdown

1. Markdown-Preview.nvim

This plugin provides a live preview of Markdown files in
your browser.

Installation:
Using `packer.nvim`:

```
lua
CopierModifier
use {
    'iamcco/markdown-preview.nvim',
    run = 'cd app && npm install',
    setup = function() vim.g.mkdp_filetypes = {
"markdown" } end,
    ft = { "markdown" },
}
```

Usage:

- Start the live preview:

```
vim
CopierModifier
:MarkdownPreview
```

- Stop the preview:

```
vim
CopierModifier
:MarkdownPreviewStop
```

2. Vim-Pandoc

Vim-Pandoc enhances Markdown editing with support for Pandoc-specific syntax and features.

Installation:
Using `packer.nvim`:

```
lua
CopierModifier
use 'vim-pandoc/vim-pandoc'
use 'vim-pandoc/vim-pandoc-syntax'
```

Key Features:

- Better syntax highlighting for Markdown and Pandoc documents.
- Integration with Pandoc for exporting to formats like PDF and HTML.

Adding Spell Check and Grammar Tools

Spell Checking in Neovim

Enable spell check for your writing:

```
vim
CopierModifier
:set spell
:set spelllang=en_us
```

- Toggle spell check:

  ```
  vim
  CopierModifier
  :set spell!
  ```

- Navigate misspelled words:

  ```
  vim
  CopierModifier
  ]s  -- Next misspelled word
  [s  -- Previous misspelled word
  ```

- Correct a misspelled word:
  Move the cursor to the word and press z= to choose
  a correction.

Grammar Tools with LSP

Use ltex-ls for grammar and style checks:

Installation:
Install ltex-ls (requires Java):

```
bash
CopierModifier
brew install ltex-ls
```

Configure in Neovim:

```lua
lua
CopierModifier
require'lspconfig'.ltex.setup{
    settings = {
        ltex = {
            language = "en-US"
        }
    }
}
```

Exporting and Previewing Markdown Files

Exporting with Pandoc

Pandoc is a powerful tool for converting Markdown files to various formats (PDF, HTML, DOCX, etc.).

1. **Install Pandoc**:

   ```bash
   bash
   CopierModifier
   sudo apt install pandoc
   ```

2. **Export to PDF**:

   ```bash
   bash
   CopierModifier
   pandoc file.md -o file.pdf
   ```

3. **Export to HTML**:

   ```bash
   bash
   CopierModifier
   pandoc file.md -o file.html
   ```

Previewing Markdown with Markdown-Preview.nvim

The `Markdown-Preview.nvim` plugin allows you to view Markdown files as they would appear on a website.

- Open the Markdown file in Neovim.
- Start the live preview:

```
vim
CopierModifier
:MarkdownPreview
```

- The file will open in your default browser with live updates as you edit.

With Neovim configured for writing and Markdown editing, you can enjoy a focused and efficient workflow. In the next chapter, we'll delve into collaborative features and techniques for working on shared documents using Neovim.

Chapter 8: Exploring Neovim for Templating and Scripting

Neovim is not just a powerful text editor; it's also a robust tool for automating workflows, templating, and scripting. This chapter will explore how you can supercharge your productivity by creating custom commands, setting up snippets, and scripting directly within Neovim.

Automating Workflows with Custom Commands

Custom commands in Neovim allow you to automate repetitive tasks and simplify complex workflows.

Defining Custom Commands

Use the :command directive to create custom commands:

```vim
CopierModifier
command! MyCommand echo "Hello, Neovim!"
```

Now you can run the custom command with:

```vim
CopierModifier
```

```
:MyCommand
```

Automating Tasks with Lua

In Neovim, Lua scripts provide greater flexibility for automation:

```lua
CopierModifier
vim.api.nvim_create_user_command('Greet',
function()
    print("Welcome to Neovim!")
end, {})
```

This creates a command `:Greet` that displays a greeting.

Setting Up Snippets for Faster Coding

Snippets are reusable templates that expand into predefined blocks of text, saving you time while coding.

Choosing a Snippet Engine

Popular snippet engines for Neovim include:

1. **LuaSnip**
2. **Ultisnips**
3. **Snippy**

LuaSnip: A Modern Snippet Engine

Installation:
Using `packer.nvim`:

```lua
```

```
CopierModifier
use 'L3MON4D3/LuaSnip'
use 'rafamadriz/friendly-snippets' -- Predefined
snippets for various languages
```

Basic LuaSnip Setup:

```
lua
CopierModifier
local ls = require("luasnip")

ls.add_snippets("lua", {
    ls.parser.parse_snippet("func", "function
$1($2)\n  $0\nend"),
})
```

Usage:

- Type `func`, then press the expansion key (e.g., `Tab`) to insert the snippet.
- Use `Tab` to navigate through placeholders.

Ultisnips: A Classic Snippet Engine

Installation:
Using `packer.nvim`:

```
lua
CopierModifier
use 'SirVer/ultisnips'
use 'honza/vim-snippets' -- Community-driven
snippets
```

Defining Snippets:
Create a snippet file in `~/.vim/UltiSnips/`:

```
snippets
CopierModifier
snippet func
function ${1:function_name}(${2:args})
```

```
  ${0}
end
endsnippet
```

Usage:

- Type `func`, press `Tab`, and the snippet expands.

Writing and Running Scripts Directly in Neovim

Neovim allows you to write and execute scripts without leaving the editor.

Running Lua Code

You can evaluate Lua code directly in Neovim:

1. Open the command line:

```
vim
CopierModifier
:lua print("Hello, Lua!")
```

2. To execute a Lua script from a file:

```
vim
CopierModifier
:luafile %
```

Running Vim Script

To execute Vim script commands, simply use the `source` command:

```
vim
CopierModifier
```

```
:source %
```

This runs the current file as a Vim script.

Automating Tasks with Scripts

Example: A Lua script to format JSON files:

```lua
CopierModifier
vim.api.nvim_create_user_command('FormatJSON',
function()
    vim.cmd('%!jq .')
end, {})
```

Run `:FormatJSON` in Neovim to format the current JSON file.

Combining Snippets and Scripting

Combine snippets and scripting for advanced templating. For example:

1. Create a snippet for a Python function:

    ```lua
    CopierModifier
    ls.add_snippets("python", {
        ls.parser.parse_snippet("def", "def
    ${1:function_name}(${2:args}):\n
    ${0}"),
    })
    ```

2. Add a script to auto-insert the snippet when starting a new Python file:

    ```lua
    ```

```
CopierModifier
vim.api.nvim_create_autocmd("BufNewFile",
{
    pattern = "*.py",
    callback = function()
        vim.cmd("lua
require'luasnip'.jump(1)")
    end,
})
```

This setup inserts a Python function template automatically in new `.py` files.

By mastering snippets, scripting, and templating, you can transform Neovim into a highly efficient environment tailored to your workflow. In the next chapter, we'll dive deeper into troubleshooting and fine-tuning your Neovim setup for maximum performance.

Chapter 9: Neovim for Remote Development

Neovim is a powerful tool for remote development, enabling you to access and edit files on remote servers seamlessly. Whether you're working over SSH, managing cloud environments, or integrating with containerized setups, this chapter will guide you through making Neovim your go-to editor for remote workflows.

Accessing Remote Servers with Neovim

Using SSH to Connect to a Remote Server

SSH (Secure Shell) is a common method for accessing remote servers.

1. **Log in to the server**:

   ```bash
   CopierModifier
   ssh username@remote-server
   ```

2. **Open Neovim on the server**:

   ```bash
   CopierModifier
   ```

```
nvim
```

3. **Edit files directly**:
   Navigate the file system and open files in Neovim as you would locally.

Using Mosh for Stable Connections

Mosh (Mobile Shell) is an alternative to SSH that offers better performance over unreliable networks.

1. **Install Mosh**:
   - o On your local machine and server:

     ```bash
     CopierModifier
     sudo apt install mosh   # For
     Debian/Ubuntu
     ```

2. **Connect to the server**:

   ```bash
   CopierModifier
   mosh username@remote-server
   ```

3. **Run Neovim** as usual after connecting.

Using Neovim with Tmux for Seamless Multitasking

Tmux (Terminal Multiplexer) enhances your remote development experience by allowing you to create, detach, and manage multiple terminal sessions.

Installing Tmux

```
bash
CopierModifier
sudo apt install tmux  # Debian/Ubuntu
```

Starting a Tmux Session

1. Create a new session:

   ```
   bash
   CopierModifier
   tmux new -s mysession
   ```

2. Run Neovim within the Tmux session:

   ```
   bash
   CopierModifier
   nvim
   ```

Benefits of Tmux + Neovim

- Detach from your session and reattach later:

  ```
  bash
  CopierModifier
  tmux detach
  tmux attach -t mysession
  ```

- Split terminal panes for multitasking:

  ```
  bash
  CopierModifier
  Ctrl-b %  # Vertical split
  Ctrl-b "  # Horizontal split
  ```

Remote File Editing with Plugins

vim-ftp

```
```

This plugin enables file editing over FTP or SFTP.

Installation:
Using `packer.nvim`:

```lua
CopierModifier
use 'tracyone/vim-ftp'
```

Basic Usage:

1. Open a remote file:

   ```vim
   CopierModifier
   :e sftp://user@remote-server/path/to/file
   ```

2. Save changes directly to the remote server:

   ```vim
   CopierModifier
   :w
   ```

rclone Integration

Rclone is a powerful tool for managing files in cloud storage.

1. **Install Rclone**:

   ```bash
   CopierModifier
   sudo apt install rclone
   ```

2. **Configure a remote connection**:

   ```bash
   CopierModifier
   rclone config
   ```

3. **Mount remote storage**:

```bash
CopierModifier
rclone mount remote: ~/remote-folder
```

4. Open files with Neovim:

```bash
CopierModifier
nvim ~/remote-folder/file.txt
```

Integrating with Cloud IDEs and Containerized Environments

Working with Docker Containers

Access and edit files in running containers directly.

1. **Exec into the container**:

```bash
CopierModifier
docker exec -it container_name bash
```

2. **Run Neovim** inside the container:

```bash
CopierModifier
nvim
```

Using Cloud IDEs with Neovim

Many cloud IDEs (e.g., GitHub Codespaces, AWS Cloud9) support Neovim integration.

1. Connect to the development environment via SSH.

2. Use Neovim to edit files as if they were local.

By combining these techniques, you can seamlessly work on remote servers, manage files in cloud storage, and integrate Neovim into your cloud-based or containerized workflows. In the next chapter, we'll focus on troubleshooting and performance optimization to ensure your Neovim setup runs smoothly in all environments.

Chapter 10: Troubleshooting and Debugging Neovim

As a powerful text editor, Neovim can sometimes present challenges when configurations, plugins, or settings don't work as expected. In this chapter, we will explore methods for troubleshooting common issues in Neovim, from configuration errors to plugin conflicts, and how to utilize built-in tools to diagnose and resolve these issues.

Debugging Configuration Errors in Neovim

Common Sources of Configuration Errors

Configuration errors in Neovim usually arise from mistakes in your `init.lua` (or `.vimrc` for Vim users), misconfigured plugins, or incompatible settings. Here are some common causes:

- **Typos or syntax errors** in your configuration file.
- **Unresolved plugin dependencies** or outdated plugins.
- **Conflicting settings** or overlapping plugins.
- **Missing or incorrect paths** for plugin or file locations.

Tips for Debugging Configuration Files

1. **Check for syntax errors**: Ensure that your Lua configuration (`init.lua`) follows correct Lua syntax, and your Vimscript-based configuration (`.vimrc`) is also error-free. Use an IDE or linter to catch syntax issues early.
2. **Isolate the issue**: If you suspect a configuration error, comment out parts of your configuration and restart Neovim to identify the problematic section. Gradually reintroduce parts of your configuration until the issue resurfaces.
3. **Use `:checkhealth`**:
   Neovim has a built-in health check that can help identify common issues with your setup. To run it:

   ```
   vim
   CopierModifier
   :checkhealth
   ```

   This will run checks for missing dependencies, outdated plugins, and other potential problems.

4. **Log errors**: If Neovim crashes or exhibits unusual behavior, checking the log file can provide valuable information about what's going wrong. The log file is typically located in `~/.local/share/nvim/log`. You can also view it directly in Neovim with:

   ```
   vim
   CopierModifier
   :e ~/.local/share/nvim/log
   ```

Using `:messages`, `:checkhealth`, and Log Files for Troubleshooting

`:messages`

The :messages command displays a history of messages that Neovim has displayed during your session. This can be particularly helpful for identifying errors or warnings.

- **Check recent error messages**:

```
vim
CopierModifier
:messages
```

  Look for any error messages that might point to configuration issues or plugin errors.

:checkhealth

The :checkhealth command runs a series of built-in checks to help diagnose potential issues in your Neovim setup. After running the command, review the output for any errors or warnings related to:

- Missing dependencies (e.g., required libraries or tools for plugins).
- Plugin-specific issues.
- Configuration problems.

If the output shows no issues, your setup is in good shape; if there are issues, the output will include suggestions for resolving them.

Resolving Conflicts Between Plugins and Settings

Plugin conflicts are one of the most common sources of issues in Neovim. These conflicts can arise due to overlapping functionality, incompatible versions, or misconfigured settings. Here's how you can resolve them:

Identifying Conflicting Plugins

To identify conflicting plugins:

1. **Disable plugins one by one**: Temporarily disable plugins in your `init.lua` file (or plugin manager configuration) and reload Neovim. Re-enable them gradually to pinpoint the conflicting plugin.
2. **Check plugin compatibility**: Some plugins may be incompatible with each other or require specific versions of Neovim. Always check the documentation for compatibility notes or issues with other plugins.
3. **Use `:checkhealth` for plugin-specific checks**: Some plugins may provide health checks themselves. For instance, LSP configurations often need specific dependencies that can be checked using `:checkhealth`.

Resolving Conflicts Between Plugin Settings

If two plugins or settings are conflicting, you can try the following methods to resolve the issue:

1. **Load order**: Plugins loaded later can sometimes override earlier ones. If you use a plugin manager (e.g., `packer.nvim`), you can change the order in which plugins are loaded. Some plugins even have specific instructions on load order in their documentation.
2. **Namespace settings**: Many plugins support custom namespaces for settings. If a conflict arises from overlapping settings, consider using different namespaces or explicitly setting variables to avoid collisions.

3. **Lazy load plugins**: For performance reasons, it's best to lazy-load plugins whenever possible. Lazy loading ensures plugins are only loaded when necessary, which minimizes the chances of conflicts during startup.

Troubleshooting Plugin Dependencies

Sometimes plugins rely on external programs or tools that may not be installed or configured correctly. To fix this:

1. **Check for missing dependencies**: Verify that all required external dependencies are installed and correctly configured. For instance, if you use a plugin like `nvim-lspconfig`, ensure that you have the necessary LSP servers installed and configured.
2. **Use the plugin manager's update function**: If you notice a plugin is outdated, updating it could resolve many issues. Run the appropriate update command based on your plugin manager (e.g., `:PackerUpdate` for `packer.nvim`).

Summary

Troubleshooting and debugging in Neovim involves a systematic approach to diagnose issues using tools like `:messages`, `:checkhealth`, and log files. By following best practices for configuration, plugin management, and debugging, you can quickly resolve common issues and keep your Neovim environment running smoothly.

Chapter 11: Taking Neovim to the Next Level

As you grow more comfortable with Neovim, it's time to push the boundaries of what you can do with this powerful editor. In this chapter, we'll explore how to elevate your Neovim experience by writing your own plugins, integrating Neovim with external tools, performing advanced search and replace operations, and sharing your custom configuration with the world.

Writing Your Own Plugins in Lua or Vimscript

One of Neovim's most powerful features is its extensibility. You can write custom plugins to enhance your workflow or tailor the editor to your specific needs.

Lua vs Vimscript for Plugin Development

Neovim supports both Lua and Vimscript for writing plugins, with Lua being the preferred language due to its higher performance and flexibility.

- **Lua**: Neovim's Lua API is fast and allows you to leverage modern programming paradigms like object-oriented or functional programming.
- **Vimscript**: Vimscript is still widely used, especially for legacy configurations, but it is slower than Lua and lacks many modern programming features.

Getting Started with Lua Plugin Development

To write your first Lua plugin, follow these steps:

1. **Create a Plugin Directory**: Plugins are typically stored in `~/.config/nvim/lua/` or `~/.local/share/nvim/site/pack/`.

2. **Create Lua Files**: Create a Lua file to define the plugin logic. For instance, `~/.config/nvim/lua/myplugin.lua`:

```lua
CopierModifier
local M = {}

function M.say_hello()
    print("Hello from my first Neovim plugin!")
end

return M
```

3. **Load Your Plugin**: To load the plugin, add the following to your `init.lua`:

```lua
CopierModifier
require('myplugin').say_hello()
```

4. **Expand the Plugin**: You can extend the plugin by adding more functionality, commands, or key mappings. Lua allows you to interact directly with Neovim's API.

Writing Plugins in Vimscript

Vimscript remains widely used in Neovim, especially for simple configurations. Here's an example of a basic Vimscript plugin:

```vim
```

```
CopierModifier
" myplugin.vim
function! MyPluginSayHello()
  echo "Hello from my Vimscript plugin!"
endfunction

command! SayHello call MyPluginSayHello()
```

To load this plugin in `init.vim`:

```
vim
CopierModifier
source ~/.config/nvim/myplugin.vim
```

Integrating Neovim with External Tools

Neovim excels at integrating with external tools, making it a versatile editor. By integrating tools like `fzf` (fuzzy finder) or `ripgrep` (fast search tool), you can supercharge your workflow.

Integrating `fzf` with Neovim

`fzf` is a command-line fuzzy finder that works seamlessly with Neovim for quick file navigation and searching. Here's how to set it up:

1. **Install `fzf`:**
   o   On Linux/macOS:

      ```
      bash
      CopierModifier
      brew install fzf
      ```

   o   On Windows, use `choco install fzf` or follow the instructions on the `fzf` GitHub page.

2. **Install `fzf.vim` Plugin**: Using your plugin manager (e.g., `packer.nvim`), install the `fzf.vim` plugin:

```lua
CopierModifier
use 'junegunn/fzf.vim'
```

3. **Using `fzf` in Neovim**:
   - Press `:Files` to open a fuzzy file finder.
   - Use `:Buffers` to switch between open buffers using fuzzy matching.

Integrating `ripgrep` with Neovim

`ripgrep` is a fast searching tool that works well with Neovim for searching files and content.

1. **Install `ripgrep`**:

```bash
CopierModifier
brew install ripgrep   # macOS
sudo apt install ripgrep   # Ubuntu/Debian
```

2. **Install `fzf` and Configure `ripgrep`**:
   - Set `ripgrep` as your default search tool in Neovim. In your `init.lua`, add:

```lua
CopierModifier
vim.g.fzf_command_prefix = 'Rg'
```

   - Now, you can use `:Rg <query>` to search files using `ripgrep`.

Advanced Search and Replace with Neovim Commands

Neovim's search and replace functionality is powerful, especially when combined with regular expressions and external tools like `ripgrep`. Here are a few advanced search techniques:

Using Regular Expressions for Search

Neovim supports Vim's regular expression syntax. For more advanced searches, you can:

- **Search for specific patterns**:

```vim
CopierModifier
/^\d\+  # Finds lines starting with a
number.
```

- **Search and replace**:

```vim
CopierModifier
:%s/old_pattern/new_pattern/g  # Replace
'old_pattern' with 'new_pattern' globally.
```

Using `:argdo` for Multiple File Replacements

You can search and replace across multiple files at once using `:argdo`:

```vim
CopierModifier
:args *.js
:argdo %s/old_value/new_value/gc
```

71

This will replace `old_value` with `new_value` in all JavaScript files.

Using External Tools for Search and Replace

You can also pipe the search and replace functionality of external tools like `sed` and `ripgrep` directly into Neovim:

```vim
CopierModifier
:!rg old_pattern -l | xargs sed -i
's/old_pattern/new_pattern/g'
```

Sharing Your Neovim Configuration on GitHub

If you've customized Neovim to suit your needs, sharing your configuration on GitHub is a great way to contribute to the community or just back up your setup.

Preparing Your Configuration for GitHub

1. **Create a Git Repository**: Initialize a Git repository in your Neovim configuration directory:

   ```bash
   CopierModifier
   cd ~/.config/nvim
   git init
   ```

2. **Add Files**: Add your `init.lua` and any other custom Lua or Vimscript files:

   ```bash
   CopierModifier
   git add init.lua lua/
   ```

3. **Commit and Push**: Commit your changes and push them to GitHub:

```bash
CopierModifier
git commit -m "Initial Neovim
configuration"
git remote add origin <your-repo-url>
git push -u origin master
```

Making Your Configuration Discoverable

Once your configuration is on GitHub:

- Add a detailed README with explanations for your setup.
- Include installation instructions for others to replicate your setup.
- Use tags or topics to make your repository easier to find.

Summary

In this chapter, we took Neovim to the next level by creating custom plugins, integrating external tools like `fzf` and `ripgrep`, and performing advanced search and replace operations. We also covered how to share your custom Neovim setup on GitHub, allowing you to contribute to the wider Neovim community.

With these advanced techniques, you'll be able to optimize your Neovim workflow and fully harness its power for both coding and general productivity.

Conclusion: Embracing the Neovim Journey

As you reach the end of this book, take a moment to reflect on the journey you've taken from a Neovim newcomer to an empowered user. You've learned how to set up and customize Neovim, integrate powerful plugins, leverage advanced features, and optimize your workflow for maximum productivity. You've gained insights into making Neovim a robust development environment, capable of handling everything from coding to writing and remote development. But this is only the beginning.

Reflecting on Your Journey from Zero to Hero

When you first picked up Neovim, the sheer scope of its capabilities and the command-line interface might have felt intimidating. Perhaps you started with a few basic commands and configurations, unsure of what lay ahead. Now, you've explored how to configure Neovim with Lua, install powerful plugins, harness the full potential of Neovim for both programming and writing, and even debug and optimize your setup.

Along the way, you've not only learned the mechanics of Neovim but also adopted a mindset of efficiency, precision, and continuous improvement. From mastering basic navigation to fine-tuning your environment with complex workflows, you've taken a significant step toward becoming a true Neovim "hero."

Remember that this transformation is a process, and with practice, the skills you've acquired will become second nature.

The Importance of Continuous Learning with Neovim

Neovim, like many tools, is constantly evolving. The Neovim community is vibrant, and new plugins, configurations, and features emerge regularly. Staying on top of these developments will ensure that you continue to make the most of this powerful editor.

Continuous learning with Neovim means:

- **Staying updated**: Keep an eye on new features, enhancements, and best practices that emerge with each Neovim update.
- **Experimenting**: Try new plugins, configurations, and workflows. Don't be afraid to explore creative ways of using Neovim.
- **Contributing**: If you develop custom plugins or configurations, consider contributing to the community by sharing your setup or even submitting to repositories like GitHub or Neovim plugin directories.

The more you invest in Neovim, the more it will reward you by becoming an increasingly indispensable part of your daily work.

Resources for Staying Updated

To stay ahead of the curve and continue evolving as a Neovim user, tap into the wealth of resources and communities that exist around this editor. Here are a few places where you can learn, ask questions, and share your knowledge:

- **Neovim GitHub Repository**: The official Neovim GitHub repository is where you'll find the latest releases, bug fixes, and detailed documentation. It's also a great place to contribute and report issues.
  - Neovim GitHub
- **Neovim Subreddit**: A vibrant community of Neovim users on Reddit where you can ask questions, share tips, and learn from others.
  - r/neovim
- **Neovim IRC and Discord Channels**: Live chat with other Neovim enthusiasts for real-time help, advice, and discussions. IRC channels like `#neovim` on Freenode and the Neovim Discord server are popular options.
- **Neovim Wiki**: The official Neovim Wiki on GitHub contains guides, tips, and examples, which are continuously updated by contributors.
  - Neovim Wiki
- **Plugin Repositories (GitHub)**: Explore, install, and contribute to Neovim plugins via GitHub. Popular repositories like `junegunn` and `nvim-lua` offer collections of high-quality plugins.
  - Awesome Neovim
- **Tutorials and Blogs**: Many developers share in-depth tutorials and insights into Neovim, helping you expand your knowledge. Popular blog platforms like Medium and Dev.to often feature Neovim-focused articles.

- **YouTube Channels**: Video tutorials are an excellent way to learn Neovim visually. Channels dedicated to Vim, Neovim, and programming in general provide step-by-step guides for setting up and mastering Neovim.

Moving Forward

As you continue to explore and push the boundaries of what Neovim can do, always keep the spirit of exploration and improvement alive. Neovim's capabilities are vast, and as you grow in your understanding, you'll find new ways to refine your workflow and improve your efficiency.

Thank you for embarking on this journey with me! Whether you're a beginner, an intermediate user, or an expert, your path with Neovim is just getting started, and there's always more to discover. Happy coding, writing, and Neovim-ing!

Appendices

Neovim Cheat Sheet for Quick Reference

This quick reference guide provides essential Neovim commands and tips to help you navigate and work efficiently in Neovim.

Basic Modes:

- **Normal mode (Esc)**: Navigate and manipulate text.
- **Insert mode (i, I, a, A)**: Enter and edit text.
- **Visual mode (v, V, Ctrl+V)**: Select text for operations.
- **Command-line mode (:)**: Execute Neovim commands.

Navigating Files:

- `:e <filename>`: Open a file.
- `:w`: Save the current file.
- `:q`: Quit Neovim.
- `:wq`: Save and quit.
- `:x`: Save and quit (alternative to `:wq`).
- `:bd`: Close the current buffer.
- `:tabnew`: Open a new tab.
- `:ls`: List open buffers.
- `:b <buffer_number>`: Switch to another buffer.

Editing Commands:

- `x`: Delete a single character.
- `dd`: Delete a line.
- `yy`: Yank (copy) a line.

- `p`: Paste after the cursor.
- `P`: Paste before the cursor.
- `u`: Undo the last change.
- `Ctrl+r`: Redo the last undone change.
- `>>`: Indent the current line.
- `<<`: Unindent the current line.

Searching:

- `/pattern`: Search forward for a pattern.
- `?pattern`: Search backward for a pattern.
- `n`: Next occurrence of the search.
- `N`: Previous occurrence of the search.
- `:noh`: Clear search highlighting.

Working with Windows:

- `Ctrl+w h/j/k/l`: Move between split windows (left, down, up, right).
- `:split <filename>`: Horizontal split.
- `:vsplit <filename>`: Vertical split.
- `:resize <number>`: Resize the current window.

Registers:

- `"a`: Access register "a" for yanked or deleted text.
- `:reg`: View all registers.

Exiting Neovim:

- `:qa`: Quit all windows.
- `:wqa`: Write and quit all windows.

Recommended Plugins and Configurations

Here are some essential plugins and configurations to enhance your Neovim experience.

1. Plugin Manager:

- **Packer.nvim**: A fast and flexible plugin manager written in Lua.
  - o `use 'wbthomason/packer.nvim'`

2. File Navigation and Searching:

- **telescope.nvim**: Powerful fuzzy finder for files, buffers, and more.
  - o `use 'nvim-telescope/telescope.nvim'`
- **fzf.vim**: Integrates fzf with Neovim for fast searching.
  - o `use 'junegunn/fzf.vim'`

3. LSP and Autocompletion:

- **nvim-lspconfig**: Configures Language Server Protocol (LSP) for multiple languages.
  - o `use 'neovim/nvim-lspconfig'`
- **nvim-cmp**: Autocompletion plugin.
  - o `use 'hrsh7th/nvim-cmp'`
- **cmp-nvim-lsp**: LSP source for nvim-cmp.
  - o `use 'hrsh7th/cmp-nvim-lsp'`

4. Syntax Highlighting:

- **treesitter.nvim**: Fast and accurate syntax highlighting.
  - o `use 'nvim-treesitter/nvim-treesitter'`

5. Git Integration:

- **fugitive.vim**: Powerful Git integration for Neovim.
  - o   use 'tpope/vim-fugitive'
- **gitsigns.nvim**: Git diff signs and staging in the gutter.
  - o   use 'lewis6991/gitsigns.nvim'

6. Status Line and Themes:

- **lualine.nvim**: A fast and customizable status line.
  - o   use 'hoob3rt/lualine.nvim'
- **gruvbox**: Popular color scheme for a clean and readable interface.
  - o   use 'morhetz/gruvbox'

7. Writing and Markdown:

- **markdown-preview.nvim**: Live preview for Markdown files.
  - o   use 'iamcco/markdown-preview.nvim'
- **vim-pandoc**: A Pandoc plugin for document conversions.
  - o   use 'vim-pandoc/vim-pandoc'

8. Snippets:

- **luasnip**: A powerful snippet engine.
  - o   use 'L3MON4D3/LuaSnip'
- **ultisnips**: Another powerful snippet engine.
  - o   use 'SirVer/ultisnips'

FAQs for Beginners and Common Errors

Q1: Neovim is not opening correctly. What should I do?

- **A1:** Ensure that Neovim is installed correctly. Try running `nvim --version` in your terminal to check if Neovim is installed. If it's not, reinstall it according to your platform's instructions.

Q2: How can I remove unwanted plugins in Neovim?

- **A2:** To remove plugins, simply delete or comment out their lines in your `init.lua` or `init.vim` file. Then, run `:PackerSync` if using Packer, or consult the plugin manager's documentation for removal commands.

Q3: How do I fix performance issues in Neovim?

- **A3:** Try disabling or lazily loading heavy plugins. Consider using the `:checkhealth` command to see if Neovim has any issues with its configuration. Optimize your configuration file by reducing unnecessary plugins and using native features.

Q4: My keybindings are not working. What should I check?

- **A4:** Ensure that there are no conflicts in your keybinding settings. Check your `init.lua` or `init.vim` file to ensure that key mappings are defined properly. Use the `:verbose map <key>` command to see where a keybinding is defined.

Q5: How do I resolve plugin conflicts?

- **A5:** If plugins are conflicting, try disabling plugins one by one to identify the culprit. Additionally, check plugin documentation for compatibility notes. Sometimes, resolving conflicts might involve altering settings or updating Neovim or the plugin.

Q6: How can I set up LSP for a programming language?

- **A6:** Install the LSP server for the language of your choice. For example, for Python, use `pyright` and configure it using `nvim-lspconfig`. Ensure that the appropriate settings are added to your `init.lua` to enable the LSP for the language.

Q7: How do I export my configuration?

- **A7:** You can share your Neovim configuration by uploading your `init.lua` or `init.vim` file and any associated plugin configurations to GitHub or any other version control platform. Be sure to include a README file with instructions for others to use your setup.

By referencing these appendices, you now have quick access to important commands, plugin recommendations, and solutions to common issues. Continue to explore, experiment, and refine your Neovim setup!

Table of contents

www.ingramcontent.com/pod-product-compliance
Lightning Source LLC
LaVergne TN
LVHW051538050326
832903LV00033B/4308